A PETIMALS Book

FROGADILLO

The Bounciest, Most Fetch-able Pet Ever. Hopefully.

Michael Andrew Fox
Illustrated by Ed Shems

*To all my friends and family who have supported
my dream of being a writer.*

Michael Andrew Fox

What kids say about the Petimals books,

"Elephitten is really funny because the boy really wants a pet and I can really connect with him. I always ask for a pet, but I never get one, so all the pets in the Petimals series are like a pet to me."
Jannel, Age 10

"Petimals is a funny series because he asks for a pet in each of the books. He gets a pet but has to get rid of it because it causes trouble."
Hailey, Age 9

"Dogopotamus is a hilarious book because he rummages around town and breaks everything. I like how he combines two animals and mixes them together, that's a creative way to come up with stuff. "
Asher, Age10 / Bryson, Age 10

"Hamstigator was both funny and interesting. It was funny because Hamstigator was swimming in the toilet. It was interesting because no one knows what he is going to do next."
Jon, Age 10

"I love the Petimals series. It really let's my imagination go wild! I will keep reading for many more years to come!"
Lila, Age 8

"I love your Petimals series. My favorite is Dogopotamus because I love dogs and I love hippos. My favorite is when Coby rides his Dogopotamus. It looks like fun!"
Kameron, Age 8

"I love all your books. I love how Hamstigator destroys the house. I love Hamstigator and Dogopotamus sooooo much. They're super funny."
Luena, Age 8

"Petimals are so funny. Petimals have many creative animals. My favorite part in Hamstigator is when he's in the toilet. My favorite part of Dogopotamus is when they play fetch."
Peyton, Age 7

"I think Elephitten is exciting. Also, Elephitten is funny and silly. Elephitten makes you laugh. Also, after you read it you want to share the experience. Elephitten is so inspiring."
McKenzie, Age 7

"Petimals stories are the best books in the world. They're really cool because Michael Andrew Fox mixes animals together and writes a whole story about the two animals. In my opinion, Elephitten is the best book."
Andrew, Age 7

A PETiMALs Book

FROGADILLO

The Bounciest, Most Fetch-able Pet Ever. Hopefully.

Michael Andrew Fox
Illustrated by Ed Shems

CONTENTS

PET PLANET

After crawling on the floor, pulling up every couch cushion and looking behind every piece of furniture, I finally find the TV remote. How does it end up behind the chair in the corner of the room every time? I blame my older brother, Zack!

I put the cushions back where they belong and plop down onto the couch. I turn on the TV, walk up to the game console and place the cartridge in until it clicks. "Pet Planet" has become my favorite game. It's the closest thing I will have to owning a pet until I convince my parents to let me have a real one. It's kind of like having a pet. Sort of.

The music starts playing and I see my little character pop up where I left him yesterday, walking our imaginary dog.

I love this game.

"Come on, boy," I say out loud. I move the controller and my character drags our little dog across the village square.

The villagers don't pay much attention as we walk, they just scurry around doing whatever they do. We walk around the lucky fountain, past Hedgehog's Pet Shop and onto Sandy Beach. As we move across the beach we leave a trail of footprints behind us in the sand. We walk out onto the short dock, stop and wait.

"Where's that silly bird?" I say out loud, frustrated.

I hate this game.

Just then, I realize my mistake. We turn around and walk over to the long dock. I see fish jumping in the water and two frogs bouncing back and forth between the lily pads. As we walk out towards the water we pass a little man fishing. He tries to talk to us, but we just keep moving. We wait at the end of the long dock and finally a bird flies over and lands in front of us.

I love this game.

The bird just sits there waiting.

"Oh rats, I need to feed the bird," I say.

I move the controller and turn my character around.

I hate this game.

We follow our footprints back over Sandy Beach to the other side of the village square. We find Hedgehog's Pet Shop and walk in.

"Excuse me," I say to the hedgehog behind the counter. "Can I buy some birdseed?"

The hedgehog scurries across the store and comes back with what looks like a handful of worms.

"Here you go," says the hedgehog as he places the squirmy pile in my hand.

I love this game.

We leave the store and begin to walk across the village square. Just then, an alarm goes off and the music stops. I notice two police dogs run out of the police station. All the villagers run and hide in their homes.

"Rats! What did I forget?" I mumble.

"You have to pay for that," says one of the police dogs.

"Come on!" I say out loud, frustrated.

The other police dog puts handcuffs on me and walks us into the police station.

A text bubble pops up over the police station: "You forgot to pay for the worms. That'll cost you one night in jail."

"Ugh. I hate this game!" I say out loud, and I toss the video game controller onto the couch.

Just then I hear the garage door open and Mom and Zack walk in. Zack's my older brother. He's 11-years old and thinks he's so cool. He has a little cardboard box in his hand and I can tell something's up because he has a stupid grin on his face.

Zack walks into the living room and looks at the game on the TV.

"You know you have to pay before you leave the pet store, Coby." Zack says.

Ugh. I just ignore the comment.

"RIBBIT"

"What's in the box?" I ask Zack.

"I got my turtles a buddy," he says.

Zack has a glass tank in his room that holds two box turtles. They are the lamest things ever. I'm sure whatever "buddy" he has for them is going to be just as lame.

Unless it's a snake that only eats box turtles.

He opens the lid and sitting in the corner of the box is a little slimy green ball with eyes.

"It's a frog," I say, not impressed.

"Yeah, he's cool, right?" Zack answers as he closes up the box.

It's actually not cool at all. Not only is a frog a lame pet, but the current pet count is now Zack, three - Coby, zero.

"Mom, why can Zack have another pet and I still have none?" I ask.

"Do you want a pet you can keep in a tank in your room?" Mom asks.

What exactly are my choices here? Turtles, fish, frogs? Lame, lame and lamer.

"Not really," I say.

"Well then, you'll just have to wait," Mom says. "You're only eight."

I look over at Zack who just shrugs and runs upstairs with his box. I follow him up the stairs and into his room. He removes the glass top off the tank, and of course, both turtles disappear into their shells. Stupid pets. Can you imagine if every time you came home, your dog would run and hide behind the couch? What's the point of that?

Zack opens the box, careful to keep his hand over the opening so his new pet can't jump out. He turns it upside down, removes his hand and let's the little green frog fall into the tank. It lands upside down on a rock and quickly flips itself over. Zack replaces the top of the tank and squats down so he's looking directly through the side glass. I squat down across from him and we both stare at Zack's newest addition to the family. The frog and the turtles are all just sitting there. Other than the frog's throat moving in and out, I would have no idea if any of the three creatures inside Zack's tank were dead or alive.

I don't get it. What's the point of having pets if they don't do anything. I look at the turtles, then at the frog, then back at the turtles. I turn towards Zack, who's excitedly staring into the tank like he's watching a cartoon.

"Lume," I mumble as I slowly back out into the hallway and make my way over to my room.

I sit down at my desk, frustrated. I can't believe Zack has another pet and I still have none. This is totally unfair. I wish I could convince Mom and Dad that I'm ready for my own pet.

I look over and notice the little grey model of Elephitten sitting on my shelf.

Elephitten was so cool! Half elephant and half kitten, created with the 3D printer that's in Zack's room. Now password protected thanks to my little experiment. That would have gone great if I hadn't brought Elephitten to school. That was my bad. I'm still doing chores around the house to pay for the sneakers I ruined that day. Ugh.

So, what exactly are my pet options at this point? Mom said I could have a pet that lives in a tank. The only problem is, nothing cool lives in a tank. Turtles and fish are boring. So are snakes and lizards. Frogs can jump, I guess that's kinda cool, but they can't chase a ball or play in the yard. I just want a pet I can play fetch with. Is that so hard to find?

3

ZACK'S TURN

Zack stares through the glass at his new pet. He hears Coby mumble something about frogs being lame, but doesn't pay too much attention. He's pretty sure Coby left, but doesn't bother to look up. He doesn't want to miss the moment when the turtles and the frog discover each other. He keeps staring through the glass. The frog just sits on the rock, its throat moving in and out. The turtles are still hiding in their shells. Any moment now, they would come out, right?

He must admit, this is a little boring, but he would never say that out loud to Coby. Coby thinks the turtles are lame and now he thinks the frog is lame. Zack thinks Coby's ideas are crazy. You can't just combine animals together and expect to come up with something cool. But, maybe you can take existing animals and add a little improvement.

Zack wonders what he would change about these turtles? It would be nice if they didn't spend so much time hiding in their shells. It would also be nice if they didn't move so slowly. Faster turtles, now that would be cool. There's no way Coby would think those were lame.

Zack sits down with a piece of paper and pencil and writes: "Speed Turtles" in big letters at the top.

4

COBY'S DRAWING BOARD

I sit at my desk, frustrated. If only there was some way that I could create an animal that lives in a tank and that I can also play with. Hmmm. I think about Zack's frog. The only way I could actually play with a frog is if it were bigger. Or if it could jump higher and chase a ball. Zack's frog kind of looks like a green, slimy ball. What if I could throw the frog and it could jump back to me. But, frogs are soft and squishy, so that probably wouldn't work. If a frog had a shell like a turtle, it wouldn't get hurt. You could toss it around and the shell would protect it. Then it could hop back to me. That would be so cool.

I grab a piece of paper and a pencil and draw a frog. Frogs are hard to draw, by the way. It looks more like a blob with legs.

I make a round head with big, bulging eyes. I give it a big mouth and a long tongue. Frogs have cool tongues they use to catch flies and insects. Then I draw a hard turtle shell on its back.

I sit back and look at my drawing, basically a frog with a hard shell. Something looks familiar about it. I think about it for a minute and all of a sudden it comes to me. I know what this is! It looks like an armadillo! This could be the perfect pet. It can live in a tank and I could actually play with it!

I go back to my drawing and make the shell on the back longer. It covers the whole body. Then I add a long, spiny tail. I drew frog legs and arms and put long fingers on the hands. I add little ears at the top of the head, and make the nose stick out a bit. Then I start a new drawing of a ball - a hard, spiny ball that matches the shell on the back of my creature.

I sit back again and admire what I've created. It's the perfect pet. Not only does it jump and live in a tank like a frog, but I can totally play with it in the back yard. It doesn't chase balls…it IS the ball! It's half frog and half armadillo!

I grab my pencil and in big letters beneath my

drawing I write: Frogadillo!

5

SMASH THE BUTTONS

This is going to be awesome. But, I'm not sure what to do now. Zack locked me out of his computer, so I can't use his 3D printer anymore. How am I going to create

Frogadillo? Then I think about my video game. I wonder what other animals are available in "Pet Planet."

I run downstairs and turn on the TV. The game loads and I choose to start a new game. The first thing I do is pick my pet. Luckily, every animal I can think of is listed in the video game. There are hundreds of them and they're listed alphabetically.

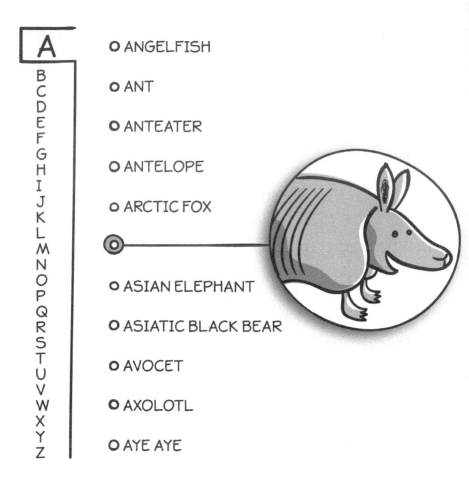

A
B
C
D
E
F
G
H
I
J
K
L
M
N
O
P
Q
R
S
T
U
V
W
X
Y
Z

○ ANGELFISH

○ ANT

○ ANTEATER

○ ANTELOPE

○ ARCTIC FOX

○ ASIAN ELEPHANT

○ ASIATIC BLACK BEAR

○ AVOCET

○ AXOLOTL

○ AYE AYE

I choose the armadillo first and then scroll down to the frog.

But, once I select frog, I lose the armadillo. With frog selected I scroll back up to the armadillo and hit the select button. The armadillo turns on and the frog turns off. I need to figure out a way to select two animals at once to create one pet.

With the armadillo selected, I scroll back down to the frog. Maybe if I hold down the "select" button and the "A" button at the same time it'll work. I try it, but nothing happens. Then I hold down "select", "A", and "B." Still nothing.

Hmmmm.

Then I decide to literally hold down every button at once. I stretch my fingers around the controller and clamp down on every button I can find. There is only one button left, but I am out of fingers. I bring the controller up to my face and with my nose I push the final button.

The game lets out a chime and on the screen

is my creation! Half frog, half armadillo.

FROGADILLO

"It worked!" I shout. "He looks just like my drawing!"

I use the controller to name my pet and spell out "Frogadillo." As soon as I hit the "start" button, my little Frogadillo character disappears.

"What happened?"

Just then the TV screen goes blank, I hear a "pop" from inside the game console and a little puff of white smoke comes out.

"Oh no!" I say out loud. "I think I just broke the game"

Zack is going to kill me when he finds out. I should just let the game rest for a while. I head upstairs to my room and as I reach the top of the stairs I hear a noise coming from behind my bedroom door. It sounds like someone's in there running around. I rush to the door and listen.

"What is that?" I wonder as I slowly reach for the doorknob.

6

SPEED TURTLES

Zack stares at the words "Speed Turtle" written at the top of the paper. He's not sure what to do next. Finally, he has an idea. He draws a rough sketch of a turtle and then he draws a little skateboard underneath the turtle.

Nah, he thought. That's not going to work.

He draws another turtle on the same sheet of paper and then a little racecar underneath the turtle. He sits back and looks

at this version.

Nope.

Zack draws a third turtle and then his best version of a little rocket strapped to the shell of the turtle.

That's more like it, Zack thinks, and he imagines how fast his new and improved turtle might go.

Zack searches through his closet for something that might work as a rocket. He goes downstairs into the basement to the far corner where there is a closed door. This is where Mom and Dad store things that we don't use everyday. Halloween costumes, Christmas decorations, beach stuff, and other random things that parents save but never actually use.

Growing up, this room was scary. There are all sorts of mechanical things in there that apparently the house needs to run. Zack's been in there before with Dad when he needed to help pack stuff away, but it's creepy. All sorts of weird noises come from that room. Crackles, whooshes, gurgles and pops that never seem to stop. But, Zack is eleven now. He can't be afraid of those things, right?

He takes two deep breaths, grabs the doorknob and with a loud squeak, pushes the door open. He steps inside and pulls a little string hanging from the ceiling that turns on the light. Once the light is on it doesn't seem so scary. He looks around at all the bins, boxes and bags organized neatly around the little storage room. He used to think Mom and Dad were nuts labeling all these boxes, but now he is glad. He rummages around and finds the box he is looking for...4th of July stuff. There must be something I can use in this box, he thinks.

He pulls the top off and searches through it. There are tons of red, white and blue streamers and little American flags, but nothing that looks like a rocket. At the very bottom he sees some old sparklers and a couple of party poppers that shoot confetti out when you pull the little string on the back.

That stuff comes out pretty fast. He grabs the poppers, puts everything back in the box, and puts the box back on the shelf. He turns the lights off and walks out, closing the door behind him.

7

FROGADILLO IS BORN

I stand outside my bedroom door and listen to the crazy noises coming from my room. It sounds like chaos in there. I grab the doorknob, turn it, and swing the door open with one quick move.

"Holy cow!" I yell, scanning the room.

My room is a mess! Everything is knocked off the shelves and clothes are everywhere. And, I can hear something under my bed. I get down on my hands and knees and press the side of my head against the carpet. I peek under – nothing there but an old sock and a weird brown ball that I haven't seen before. I push the sock to the side and reach for the brown ball.

Just as my fingers touch it, it rolls away

from me. I scootch closer and reach out again.

This time, when my fingers touch the ball it

rolls all the way to the other side of the bed.

"What the heck is going on?" I get up

and walk over to the other side.

I get down on the floor again and reach under the bed. My fingers touch the brown ball for a third time and as they do, the ball takes off! It darts around the room, flying everywhere and bouncing off the walls.

It continues to knock stuff off shelves and even starts knocking pictures off the walls.

I jump up and back into the corner of the room as the ball bounces all around and finally stops on top of my bed. It sits there for a second and then the most incredible thing happens - the ball grows legs! It starts to unravel and all of a sudden I see a little spiny tail pop out one side. From the other side I see an ear, then a nose, and then a whole head!

I take a step forward to get a closer look, and then I realize what it is. The ball isn't a ball at all! It's an animal. It's MY animal! I run over to my desk but everything has been knocked onto the floor. Under the desk I find the piece of paper with "Frogadillo" written at the top. The rest of the page is blank!

"No way!" I say as I look back and forth between the blank paper in my hand and the creature on my bed.

Just then, the creature hops up into the air, turns into a ball again and rolls over to my feet. It turns back into the 4-legged animal right in front of my eyes. I reach out and it hops into my arms. I study it closely from all angles and I can't believe what I am seeing. It matches the picture I drew perfectly. It is

Frogadillo! And it's alive!

CALENDAR?
WHAT CALENDAR?

With the party poppers in his hand, Zack runs up to his room and shuts the door. He walks over to the tank and sees the frog and the turtles just sitting there doing nothing. He stares at them for a while and reaches down and grabs one of the turtles. Just as he picks it up, he hears Mom yell from downstairs.

"Zack, let's go! We're leaving in ten minutes," Mom yells from the bottom of the stairs.

"Leaving? Where arc we going?" Zack mumbles to himself.

Zack puts the turtle back on the fake rock in the tank and runs over to the calendar that's hanging on his wall. Each month is a printed piece of paper that hangs on two

hooks attached to a wooden frame. Mom
made these two years ago as a way for us to
know what's going on each day.

As the schedules change, Mom adds or
subtracts things using her computer, prints

four copies of the updated version, and replaces four calendars around the house. One in each of our rooms, one on the refrigerator and one in the office. No matter how often she does this or how accurate the calendars are, the only one that seems to look at them is her.

"Bowling with Brent?" Zack says. "I don't want to go bowling."

Zack walks over to his bedroom door and pokes his head out.

"Mom, do I have to bowl?" Zack yells down the hallway.

"I guess not," Mom yells back. "But you still have to come with us. You can't stay here by yourself."

Zack walks back into his room and goes over to the tank. Suddenly he has an idea. He grabs one of his turtles and places it inside his backpack. He grabs the party poppers and throws them in as well. He goes over to his desk, searches through a few drawers and finds some tape. He tosses that inside, throws the backpack over his shoulder and runs out the door.

9

FETCH YOURSELF

I hear Zack running across the hall towards the stairs, but I have no idea where he's going. I peek out my bedroom door and wait for him to get downstairs. I grab Frogadillo, run downstairs through the kitchen and out the back door. I can't wait to see what Frogadillo can do. I run past Mom as she's doing something in the kitchen. As I do, I tuck Frogadillo under my arm like a football so Mom can't see it, just in case she might not approve of my newest pet creation.

"I'll be out back," I say as I reach the back door.

"Wait Coby!" Mom yells.

What?? Did she see what I had under my arm? She must have that Mom X-ray vision.

"Yeah Mom?" I ask.

"Don't be out too long," she says. "We're leaving in ten minutes."

"Ok Mom."

Phew, that was close. I guess she didn't see Frogadillo after all. Wait, leaving in ten minutes? Leaving for where?

I don't know about you, but I never know what's going on at any given moment in the day. Our days are always filled with stuff, but I never seem to know what we're doing ahead of time. I wish there was a way that all of this stuff could be written down on a single piece of paper with the days and times on it. I wonder if something like that actually exists.

"Nah," I say out loud as I shake my head and run into the backyard.

I take Frogadillo out from under my arm and look at him again. He's stretched out and looks up at me with those cute bulging eyes.

"Let's try a little test first," I say.

I try to squeeze Frogadillo back into a ball, but he doesn't budge. I flip him over onto his back and squeeze again. Still nothing.

"I need you to turn into a ball," I say.

Frogadillo just stares up at me as his tongue flicks out for a second. I spin him all around in my hands trying to figure out how to get him into a ball shape.

Maybe it's a command. Like training a dog.

"Become a ball," I yell while looking at Frogadillo.

Nothing.

"Go round!" I yell.

Nothing.

"Armadillo power!"

Still nothing. Frogadillo just stares back at me.

"Roly poly! Ball-a-rama! Bounce-a-licuous!"

No matter what I yell, Frogadillo will NOT turn into a ball. Maybe if I spin him around in my hands fast enough, he'll turn into a ball. I start to spin him as fast as I can, but nothing's happening. Just as I'm about to stop, he slips out of my hands and falls. Right before he hits the ground, he turns into a ball as he lands in the grass. I pick him back up and examine him. He's a perfect ball shape. His hard shell is wrapped around him so tight that I can barley see the legs, tail and head.

Hmmm, I guess all I had to do was drop him on the ground.

I gently toss Frogadillo in the grass again. He rolls to a stop and I see the legs, tail and head pop out. He hops up in the air and turns back into a ball as I reach out and catch him.

"So cool!" I say. "Let's try a little further"

I roll Frogadillo a few feet in front of me this time. Frogadillo unfolds, takes 2 hops towards me and flies through the air and back into my arms, landing in the shape of a ball. I decide to try a little further this time. I throw Frogadillo at least 20 feet across the yard and watch him bounce and roll to a stop. He quickly hops back towards me, launches himself into the air, turns back into a ball and lands right in my arms.

"This is the coolest pet ever!" I say.

I decide to throw Frogadillo as far across the yard as I can. He bounces and rolls all the way to our back fence. Without even a pause, he immediately hops back to me. I repeat the same throw five more times and each time Frogadillo hops back.

"This is awesome!" I yell.

I continue to throw Frogadillo across the yard for the next 10 minutes and watch him hop back to me each time. I'm amazed at what he can do. I've actually created a pet that fetches itself!

Just then I hear the back door open and Mom steps out onto the porch. I tuck Frogadillo under my arm again.

"Time to go, Coby," she yells. "Come on inside."

"Where are we going?" I ask.

"Coby, we just talked about this yesterday," Mom says as she walks back inside. "Why don't you look at one of the calendars for a change."

"Calendar?" I ask myself. "What calendar?"

I follow her into the house and walk over to the refrigerator. There, attached to the fridge by a magnet, is a single piece of paper with dates and times on it.

"Oops," I say to myself. I guess this thing actually does exist.

I look at today's date and look at the time. I see a little notation that says, "Bowling with Brent."

Brent is my best friend and lives up the street and apparently I'm going bowling with him today.

I start to walk away but then I remember what's tucked under my arm. I look down at Frogadillo and then back at the calendar and see the word "bowling," and I get a great idea!

"Coby, let's go." Mom yells from the front door. "We're meeting Brent at his house and then biking to the bowling alley together."

"Coming, Mom," I say.

I grab my helmet and backpack, stuff Frogadillo inside and run out to the garage.

10

BOWLING BONANZA

As soon as we walk inside the bowling alley, I start getting excited. There's just something cool about a bowling alley. The first thing I notice is the smell. It's a combination of rental shoe spray and fried

food. Yummy!

Then you can't help but notice the noises. Balls rolling across hardwood lanes, bowling pins crashing, people talking or cheering. There's also an arcade that makes tons of noises. Bells and whistles are going off constantly.

I'm not really paying attention as we walk over to the front desk where you get your shoes, but once I look up my heart sinks. It's Brooke, Brent's older sister. Brooke and Brent's parents actually own the bowling alley and Brooke works behind the desk, handing out rental shoes and giving out quarters to the kids playing arcade games. She doesn't like me very much. I'm always hanging out with Brent at his house and messing with Brooke's stuff. We're not allowed to go in her room, but something always happens and we end up in there and we usually break something.

"Hi Brooke!" Mom says, excited to see her.

"Hi guys!" Brooke says to Mom and Zack with a smile. Then the smile goes away and without even looking at me says, "Lane five, Coby. Here are your shoes."

Brooke hands me the oldest and dirtiest

pair of bowling shoes I've ever seen.

The sides are tattered and worn, and the

color looks like rust. I didn't think shoes

could actually rust, but it looks like these might have. The laces are frayed and they're tied in so many knots that even a magician couldn't get these untied. These might be the first pair of rental shoes in the history of bowling.

"Thanks a lot," I say as I gently pick up the shoes by the laces, trying not to touch any other part of them.

I make my way over to lane five where I see Brent putting on sparkly new bowling shoes. Figures. Brent is here all the time since his parents own the place. And, he's an amazing bowler. I've never beaten him once. But today, that's all going to change.

I force my feet into the bowling shoes since I can't untie them. Once my feet are in, they actually fit ok. We wait as Brooke puts all the names into the electronic scoring system that's up on the TV monitor above the alley. I see Brent's name pop up, then Mom, then I see what's supposed to be my name. Instead she mixed up the letters and it says, "Bocy." I glance over towards Brooke and she has a smirk on her face.

The lights turn on down by the pins and that means we're ready to go. This bowling alley has two different types of bowling. There are the normal balls with the big, white pins that the adults use, but they also have the smaller balls with thin, smaller pins for the kids. I think they call them candlepins or duckpins or something like that. Those are the ones we're using today.

Brent goes first. He grabs a ball from the ball return, lines up, and throws it down the lane. It rolls straight down the alley but towards the end it slides a little right. It still knocks down 7 pins, but Brent is not happy.

"Rats!" Brent says.

"Try throwing it down the middle next time," I say, smiling.

"Shut up, Bocy!" Brent says with a grin.

I'm going to kill Brooke.

Even though there are plenty of balls in the ball return, Brent stands there waiting for the same ball he threw the first time to come back. It finally spits out of the ball return with a clunk, and he grabs it and sets up again. He throws the ball down the alley and this time the ball fades to the left and he knocks down the remaining 3 pins.

"Sweet!" Brent says as he sits down with a smile on his face.

"Mom's turn," I say.

Mom's a good bowler. I've never beaten her either. She grabs a ball, sets up and rolls it down the lane. It's not going very fast, but it's straight. It hits the front pin and knocks most of them down. There are only 2 left. Instead of waiting for that ball to come back like Brent, she just grabs the next one in line, sets up again and rolls it down the lane. It knocks both pins down.

"Yes!" Mom shouts, as she walks back towards us. "Your turn Coby."

"One second," I say as I reach inside my backpack and grab Frogadillo. I hide him under my arm as I walk up towards the lane. I pretend to grab a ball from the ball return, but instead I pull Frogadillo out from under my arm. I gently drop him on the ground in front of me as I watch him turn into a ball right before my eyes. I pick him up, turn towards the pins at the end of the lane and hold Frogadillo right up to my face.

"I'm going to roll you down the lane and you knock all those pins down, Ok?" I whisper to Frogadillo.

I have no idea if he heard me or not, but here goes nothing. I slide forward, swing Frogadillo back and forth and launch him down the lane. He rolls down towards the pins and right before he gets there, I see him open up and he smashes into all the pins at once. Pins go flying everywhere and once they settle I see that he's knocked every

single one of them down.

"Yay!" I say as I pump my fist on the way back to my seat.

Both Mom and Brent are speechless. They are staring at me with their mouths open, shocked that I just got a strike.

"Wow, Coby!" Mom finally says. "How did you do that?"

I just shrug my shoulders, smile and sit down. I look over towards the ball return and I see that Frogadillo has come back and he's waiting patiently with the other balls in the return. Brent goes again and ends up with an eight. Mom goes and she gets a nine. Then it's my turn again.

I walk up and grab Frogadillo.

"Same as last time," I whisper.

I roll him down the lane, but he's not quite in the middle. He's drifting a little to the left. He hits most of the pins, but I see two that he misses. One on the far left and one on the far right. The dreaded split!

"Oh no," I say as I see the two pins on either side of the lane wobble back and forth.

"Ha, I knew he couldn't get two strikes in a row," Brent says from behind me. He looks relieved.

As I watch the pins wobble back and forth, I notice Frogadillo at the very end of the alley behind all the fallen pins.

"Too bad, Coby." Brent says as he gets up for his turn.

I look more closely down the lane, and I catch Frogadillo's eyes. I know it's far away but I swear I see him wink at me.

Suddenly, he opens his mouth and I see his tongue whip out and knock over both pins. It happens so fast that if I blinked my eyes, I would have missed it!

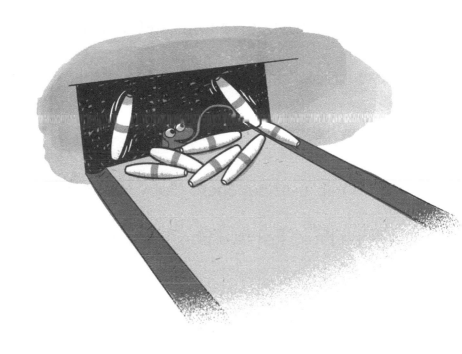

"What the….?" Brent says, astonished.

"Another strike!" I exclaim as I do a double fist pump and walk past him to my seat.

This time both Mom and Brent have confused looks on their faces. I think they're more suspicious than shocked.

"What just happened, Coby? Mom asks. "How did those last two pins fall down?"

Phew. They didn't see Frogadillo's tongue shoot out.

"Just lucky I guess," I say as I walk back.

Mom and Brent look at each other, then back at me. They know something's up, but neither knows exactly what. Finally, they just decide to go again and then it's my turn. I

grab Frogadillo and roll him down the alley.

This time, right down the middle. Another

strike! I might be the first 8-year old in the

history of bowling to bowl a perfect game.

It's almost too easy.

(11)

TURTLE POPPERS

Zack isn't interested in bowling at all.
He knows this will be the perfect place to
perform his experiment. While Mom, Coby
and Brent are bowling on lane five, Zack

grabs his backpack and walks all the way over to the furthest lane in the bowling alley. The closest bowlers to him are at least 10 lanes away and the lights are turned down on this part of the alley. Nobody will even notice him.

He grabs the turtle out of his backpack and sets him up in line with the bowling lane. Then he grabs one of the party poppers and the tape. He carefully places the party popper on the shell with the opening facing back and the string you pull facing forward. With one hand on the popper, he uses his other hand to pull out a small piece of tape to stick the popper to the shell. He rips off three more pieces of tape and uses them to secure the popper to the turtle shell.

He gives the popper a little tug just to test it and is convinced that it's secure.

"Experiment number one," Zack says to himself. "One party popper on back of turtle shell."

The turtle sticks it's head outside the shell for a quick peek and immediately disappears as if he knows what's about to happen. Zack stands off to the side, reaches down and grabs the party popper string, and starts his countdown.

"Five...four...three...two...one..." he says.

Zack pulls the string and the party popper explodes colored confetti out the back. The turtle rocks from side to side but doesn't move forward at all.

"Hmmmm," Zack says. "I guess I need more power.

Zack reaches into his backpack and grabs four more party poppers.

"Experiment number two," Zack says as he attempts to attach all four party poppers to the top of the turtle shell.

12

FROGADISASTER

After five strikes in a row, both Mom and Brent are now getting a little mad. They have NO idea how I'm doing it, and they' pretty sure I'm up to something. I step the sixth time with Frogadillo in my hand. I look down and Frogadillo opens his eyes and looks up at me with a weird look. He's cute, so I wink back at him. He closes his eyes as I swing my arm back and roll him down the lane. He gets about halfway down and all of a sudden I see him jump over to the left, landing directly in the next lane. He rolls down and smashes into the pins in the other lane.

The girl in the next lane turns and says, ey! Keep it in your own lane."

"Sorry," I say as I wait for Frogadillo to

come back through the ball return.

As soon as he shows up, I quickly grab him and walk back over to our lane. Mom and Brent have even weirder looks on their faces this time. Now they're even more convinced that I'm up to something. I line up to take another shot with Frogadillo in my hand.

"Stay in OUR lane," I whisper to Frogadillo as I swing my arm and roll him down the lane.

Frogadillo gets halfway down and this ime he hops over into the lane to my right 'nocks down all of those pins. A Dad was just about to bowl in that lane and he looks over at me.

"Hey kid, you need to keep the balls in your own lane," he says.

"I'm so sorry. I have no idea how that happened."

As soon as Frogadillo rolls into the ball return, I grab him and quickly walk back over to my lane.

I hold Frogadillo up close to my face and whisper, "What's going on Frogadil You have to stay in our lane."

I don't even bother to look back at Mom and Brent. I know they're going to start asking questions soon. I line up Frogadillo one more time and cross my fingers.

"Remember, stay in our lane," I whisper to him.

It looks good as he rolls towards the pins, but right before he gets to the end he hops into the next lane again and knocks over the pins. Then, instead of just coming back through the ball return, Frogadillo hops into her lane and knocks those pins over. He 'pping all the way down the bowling alley, knocking everyone's pins down. It looks like a crazy rubber ball has been let loose in the bowling alley.

"Oh no," I say as I watch in horror as Frogadillo rolls, hops and bounces into all the lanes, knocking down everyone's pins.

Once Frogadillo gets to the end of the bowling alley, he bounces off the wall and starts coming back the other way. This time he heads towards the top of each alley, knocking balls off the ball returns. Then he bounces behind us and starts knocking

tables, sending food and drinks flying

everywhere.

He bounces behind the check-in counter

t as Brooke ducks her head. Bowling shoes

come launching out from behind the counter as Brooke runs out screaming.

Then he bounces into the little arcade. It sounds like a giant pinball machine as k̲ come running out. People are ͬ everywhere as Frogadillo continue the bowling alley. Mom and Brent come running over to me.

"Coby…What did you do?" Mom demands.

"What is that thing?" Brent asks. "I knew you were up to something! Nobody gets five strikes in a row."

"Don't worry, I'll take care of it," I say as I run towards the far end of the bowling alley to try to catch Frogadillo.

(13)

BROOKE'S NIGHTMARE

Zack is so focused on getting all four party poppers taped to the top of the turtle shell that he doesn't notice the chaos going down at the other end of the bowling

He carefully stacks the poppers two-by-two on his turtle's shell and tapes all the strings together so that he will only have to pull one.

"This is definitely going to work," Zack says to himself as he steps back to look at his creation. "Rocket Turtle! There's no way Coby can make fun of this."

The turtle pokes his little head out from inside his shell just for a second. Even he knows this is a bad idea.

In all the chaos, Brooke is running ⌐ trying to pick up bowling balls and shoes from off the floor. Frogadillo continues to bounce all over the place as people go running in every direction. Brooke notices Zack all by himself at the other end of the bowling alley and runs over to see if he can help.

"Experiment number 2," Zack says. "Four party poppers on turtle shell."

Zack grabs the string that's connected to all four party poppers.

"Five…four…three…two…one!" he says.

Just as Zack gets to the number one, Brooke runs up right behind him and the turtle. Zack pulls the string and with a loud bang, all four party poppers go off and cover Brooke with colored confetti and streamers. Brooke screams as Zack looks up in shock.

"Oh no," Zack groans as he sees Brooke.

14

THE RACE HOME

I run towards the other end of the bowling alley as Frogadillo bounces his way in the same direction. Just as Frogadillo ___hes the last lane, I hear a scream and see what looks like a confetti explosion towards the top of the lane. At the same time I see an object fly down the lane just as Frogadillo gets there. Frogadillo and the other object collide and both come to a rest in the gutter halfway down the lane.

I run over and grab Frogadillo before he takes off again. Sitting in the gutter next to Frogadillo is what looks like one of Zack's ⌐rtles. Zack comes running towards us with ⌐cited look on his face.

"It worked!" Zack exclaims as he reaches us.

Zack picks up his turtle.

"He looks OK," Zack says as he inspects the turtle from all sides.

"What is that?" I ask.

"Rocket Turtle," Zack says proudly

"Wow, that's pretty cool," I say. "You totally saved me. Rocket Turtle stopped Frogadillo!"

"Froga-what?" Zack asks.

"Never mind, I'll tell you later," I say as I stuff Frogadillo into my backpack, grab my helmet and run out the door.

I jump on my bike and pedal as fast as I can towards home.

"I don't know if it's going to work, but I have to get to the video game before Mom and Zack get home," I say to myself, out of breath.

As I go, my feet keep slipping off the pedals and I can't figure out why. I look n and notice that I'm still wearing those disgusting, tatty bowling shoes. I also notice that the right shoe is starting to fall apart. Then I see that the left shoe is falling apart as well. Before I know it, both shoes are completely shredded. By the time I turn onto my street, the shoes are gone and now I'm just wearing socks.

I get to our driveway, dump my bike and run inside as fast as I can. I turn on the TV, hoping the video game still works. I cross my fingers and turn on the game console. The light comes on and it starts to boot up.

"Yes!" I say as I watch the lights on the front blink.

As I wait, I can hear Frogadillo inside my backpack starting to get restless.

"Come on, hurry up!" I beg.

Finally, the video game boots up and I launch the main menu of Pet Planet. I find the saved game that I titled "Frogadillo," but the picture of the character is still missing. I use the controller and scroll down to where it says, "delete." I push the "select" button and wait as the progress bar slowly crawls across the screen. As I'm waiting, I hear the garage door open.

"Oh no, please hurry," I say to the video game as the progress bar gradually makes its ay towards 100 percent. I hate this game!

Just as the door to the garage flies open, the video game finishes deleting the game. I turn towards the door and I see Mom, Zack, and Brent all staring at me. Behind them is Brooke. She's still covered in confetti and streamers and looks really mad.

Mom looks down and notices my feet.

"Coby!" Mom says with a mad tone. "Where are the rental bowling shoes?"

I look down and remember that I'm just wearing socks and the shoes are in piec between here and the bowling alley. I just sheepishly shrug my shoulders.

"You're going to pay for those," Brooke says angrily.

Then Mom says, "Coby, give me the backpack."

I gently pick up my backpack from the floor and hand it to Mom. She unzips it, looks inside and then up at me with an angry look on her face.

I just put my head down. I'm so ¹ed. I close my eyes and wait for my punishment. But nobody says anything. I look

up and I see Mom, Zack, Brent and Brooke

all staring down at the backpack. I walk over

to join the group and peek inside. A smile

comes over my face as I realize what they're

all looking at. The backpack is completely

empty.

I turn around and look over at the TV. The main menu of Pet Planet is on the screen and the little image of Frogadillo has returned to the list of characters.

I love this game!

THE END

P.S.
No turtles were hurt in
the making of this book! please
don't strap rockets to your pets!

Zack
and
Coby

Check out the other Petimals books:
Dogopotamus, Hamstigator & Elephitten!

Available NOW at:

ABOUT THE AUTHOR

Michael Andrew Fox is an Emmy Award winning television producer and author. Inspired by his own two boys, Michael rekindled his passion for writing with his children's book series, Petimals. Frogadillo is the forth book in the series.

Michael lives in Colorado with his wife, Eileen and two boys, Zack and Coby.

Visit his website: **www.petimalsbooks.com**

ABOUT THE ILLUSTRATOR

Ed Shems has been illustrating since 1991. Since graduating from the Rhode Island School of Design, Ed has illustrated more than 25 books and is currently writing and illustrating his own stories.

Visit his website: **www.edfredned.com**